# Dips

## Recipes to make your own gifts

Use these recipes to delight your friends and family. Each recipe includes gift tags for your convenience — just cut them out and personalize!

After personalizing your tag, fold and attach it to the top of the bag (above the sealed strip). Attach the tag with staples, or for a more decorative gift in a bag, use raffia, ribbon, twine, yarn or string. To do this, punch one or more holes in the top of your bag and tag at the same time. Then secure the tag using the raffia, ribbon, twine, yarn or string.

These gifts should keep for up to six months.

### Chive & Garlic Dip

1 pkg. Chive & Garlic Dip Mix
3 C. sour cream

Combine the Chive & Garlic Dip Mix with the sour cream. Stir until well blended. Cover and refrigerate. Chill at least 2 hours before serving. Serve with chips or raw vegetables.

D1040501

Printed in China

Distributed By:

507 Industrial Street
Waverly, IA 50677

ISBN 1-56383-139-2

# Chive & Garlic Dip Mix

4 tsp. dried chives
2 tsp. minced onion
1 tsp. garlic salt
1 tsp. garlic powder
1 tsp. celery seed
Pinch pepper

Combine the above ingredients and stir until well blended. Place in a 3" x 4" ziplock bag and seal.

Attach a gift tag with the directions on how to prepare the dip.

# Chive & Garlic Dip

1 pkg. Chive & Garlic Dip Mix
3 C. sour cream

Combine the Chive & Garlic Dip Mix with the sour cream. Stir until well blended. Cover and refrigerate. Chill for at least 2 hours before serving. Serve with chips, crackers or fresh vegetables.

❀ Fill a gift basket with dip mixes, crackers, chips or pretzels and a movie, cards or a board game. ❀

# Herb Veggie Dip Mix

1 T. dried parsley
1 T. dried thyme
1 1/2 tsp. dried tarragon
1 1/2 tsp. minced onion
3/4 tsp. garlic powder
1/8 tsp. salt
1/8 tsp. pepper

Combine the above ingredients and stir until well blended. Place in a 3" x 4" ziplock bag and seal.

Attach a gift tag with the directions on how to prepare the dip.

# Herb Veggie Dip

1 pkg. Herb Veggie Dip Mix
2 C. sour cream
2 tsp. lemon juice

Combine the Herb Veggie Dip Mix with the sour cream and lemon juice. Stir until well blended. Cover and refrigerate for at least 4 hours before serving. Serve with assorted fresh vegetables.

# Dill Dip Mix

2 1/2 tsp. dried dill weed
2 1/2 tsp. minced onion
2 1/2 tsp. dried parsley
1 1/2 tsp. Spice Islands® Beau
Monde Seasoning

Combine the above ingredients and stir until well blended. Place in a 3" x 4" ziplock bag and seal.

Attach a gift tag with the directions on how to prepare the dip.

# Dill Dip

1 pkg. Dill Dip Mix
1 C. mayonnaise or salad dressing
1 C. sour cream or low-fat yogurt

Combine the Dill Dip Mix with the mayonnaise and sour cream. Stir until well blended. Cover and refrigerate for at least 4 hours before serving. Serve with assorted fresh vegetables or as a topping for baked potatoes.

# Dill Dip

1 pkg. Dill Dip Mix
1 C. mayonnaise or salad dressing
1 C. sour cream or low-fat yogurt

Combine the Dill Dip Mix with the mayonnaise and sour cream. Stir until well blended. Cover and refrigerate for at least 4 hours before serving. Serve with assorted fresh vegetables or as a topping for baked potatoes.

❀ For a fall party, serve dips in small hollowed-out pumpkins. Line the inside with plastic wrap before adding the dip. ❀

- - - - - - - - - fold - - - - - - - - -

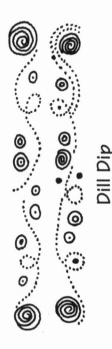

## Dill Dip

1 pkg. Dill Dip Mix
1 C. mayonnaise or salad dressing
1 C. sour cream or low-fat yogurt

Combine the Dill Dip Mix with the mayonnaise and sour cream. Stir until well blended. Cover and refrigerate for at least 4 hours before serving. Serve with assorted fresh vegetables or as a topping for baked potatoes.

To garnish with cucumber springs, cut the cucumber into 3" pieces. Poke a wooden chopstick through the center and then cut to the center until the knife hits the chopstick. Continue turning and cutting around the cucumber. Remove chopstick and gently pull the ends to form a spring.

- - - - - fold - - - - -

# Ranch Dip Mix

3/4 T. dried parsley
1 1/2 tsp. salt
3/4 tsp. dried chives
1/2 tsp. dried oregano
1/2 tsp. dried tarragon
3/4 tsp. garlic powder
3/4 tsp. lemon pepper

Combine the above ingredients and stir until well blended. Place in a 3" x 4" ziplock bag and seal.

Attach a gift tag with the directions on how to prepare the dip.

# Ranch Dip

1 pkg. Ranch Dip Mix
1 C. mayonnaise or salad dressing
1 C. sour cream

Combine the Ranch Dip Mix with the mayonnaise and sour cream. Stir until well blended. Cover and refrigerate for at least 2 hours before serving. Serve with chips, crackers or fresh vegetables.

# Parmesan Herb Dip Mix

2 T. Parmesan cheese
1 T. dried parsley
1 tsp. minced onion
1 tsp. sugar
1/4 tsp. dried oregano
1/4 tsp. dried basil
1/4 tsp. dried thyme
1/4 tsp. garlic powder
1/8 tsp. pepper

Combine the above ingredients and stir until well blended. Place in a 3" x 4" ziplock bag and seal.

Attach a gift tag with the directions on how to prepare the dip.

# Parmesan Herb Dip

1 pkg. Parmesan Herb Dip Mix
1 C. mayonnaise or salad dressing
1 C. sour cream

Combine the Parmesan Herb Dip Mix with the mayonnaise and sour cream. Stir until well blended. Cover and refrigerate. Dip is better if made 8 hours before serving. Serve with chips, crackers or fresh vegetables.

# Oniony Party Dip Mix

4 tsp. beef bouillon granules
2 T. minced onion
1/8 tsp. garlic powder
1 tsp. dried chives
1 tsp. dried parsley
1/2 tsp. powdered onion

Combine the above ingredients and stir until well blended. Place in a 3" x 4" ziplock bag and seal.

Attach a gift tag with the directions on how to prepare the dip.

# Oniony Party Dip

1 pkg. Oniony Party Dip Mix
2 C. sour cream

Combine the Oniony Party Dip Mix with the sour cream. Stir until well blended. Cover and refrigerate for at least 1 hour before serving. Serve with chips, crackers or fresh vegetables.

❀ *For a different gift, put three or four dip mixes in a decorative bowl, handmade pottery or a crystal dish.* ❀

# Fruit Dip Mix

1/3 C. brown sugar
1 T. chopped crystallized ginger
1 tsp. cinnamon

Process the above ingredients in food processor until ginger is finely chopped and mixture is well blended. Place in a 3" x 4" ziplock bag and seal.

Attach a gift tag with the directions on how to prepare the dip.

# Fruit Dip

1 pkg. Fruit Dip Mix
2 (8 oz.) pkgs. cream cheese, softened

Combine the Fruit Dip Mix with the softened cream cheese. Beat until well blended. Cover and refrigerate for 1 hour to allow flavors to blend. Serve with fresh fruit cut into bite-size pieces.

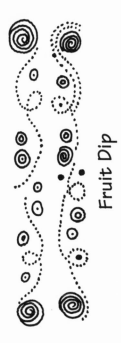

## Fruit Dip

1 pkg. Fruit Dip Mix
2 (8 oz.) pkgs. cream cheese, softened

Combine the Fruit Dip Mix with the softened cream cheese. Beat until well blended. Cover and refrigerate for 1 hour to allow flavors to blend. Serve with fresh fruit cut into bite-size pieces.

Garnish with strawberry fans. To make, start at the tip and cut the strawberry into thin slices without cutting through the end. Spread slices open to form a fan.

- - - - - - - - fold - - - - - - - - -

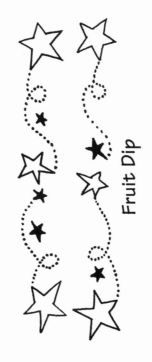

# Fruit Dip

1 pkg. Fruit Dip Mix
2 (8 oz.) pkgs. cream cheese, softened

*Combine the Fruit Dip Mix with the softened cream cheese. Beat until well blended. Cover and refrigerate for 1 hour to allow flavors to blend. Serve with fresh fruit cut into bite-size pieces.*

Serve fruit dips in hollowed-out fruits, such as pineapple, orange, grapefruit or melon halves.

- - - - - fold - - - - - - - -

# Italian Dip Mix

4 T. Parmesan cheese
2 1/2 tsp. garlic powder
2 1/2 tsp. onion powder
2 1/2 tsp. paprika
2 tsp. celery seeds
2 1/2 tsp. sesame seeds

Combine the above ingredients and stir until well blended. Place in a 3" x 4" ziplock bag and seal.

Attach a gift tag with the directions on how to prepare the dip.

# Italian Dip

1 pkg. Italian Dip Mix
2 C. sour cream

Combine the Italian Dip Mix with the sour cream. Stir until well blended. Cover and refrigerate for at least 2 hours before serving. Serve with chips, crackers or fresh vegetables.

# Mexican Fiesta Dip Mix

1 T. chili powder
2 tsp. dried parsley
1 tsp. sugar
1/2 tsp. plus 1/8 tsp. garlic powder
1/4 tsp. plus 1/8 tsp. onion powder
1/4 tsp. plus 1/8 tsp. dried cilantro
1/8 heaping tsp. cayenne pepper
1/8 heaping tsp. pepper
1/8 heaping tsp. salt

Combine the above ingredients and stir until well blended. Place in a 3" x 4" ziplock bag and seal.

Attach a gift tag with the directions on how to prepare the dip.

# Mexican Fiesta Dip

1 pkg. Mexican Fiesta Dip Mix
1 C. mayonnaise or salad dressing
1 C. sour cream

Combine the Mexican Fiesta Dip Mix with the mayonnaise and sour cream. Stir until well blended. Cover and refrigerate. Dip is better if made 8 hours before serving. Serve with chips, crackers or fresh vegetables.

# Sesame Cheese Dip Mix

2 T. Parmesan cheese
1 tsp. salt
1/8 tsp. pepper
4 tsp. toasted sesame seeds*
1 tsp. celery seed
1/4 tsp. garlic powder

Combine the above ingredients and stir until well blended. Place in a 3" x 4" ziplock bag and seal.

Attach a gift tag with the directions on how to prepare the dip.

*To toast sesame seeds, microwave for 30 seconds.

# Sesame Cheese Dip

**1 pkg. Sesame Cheese Dip Mix**
**2 C. sour cream**

Combine the Sesame Cheese Dip Mix with the sour cream. Stir until well blended. Cover and refrigerate for at least 1 hour before serving. Serve with chips, crackers or fresh vegetables.

# Bacon Dip Mix

4 T. bacon bits
2 tsp. beef bouillon granules
2 T. minced onion
1/4 tsp. minced garlic

Combine the above ingredients and stir until well blended. Place in a 3" x 4" ziplock bag and seal.

Attach a gift tag with the directions on how to prepare the dip.

# Bacon Dip

1 pkg. Bacon Dip Mix
2 C. sour cream

Combine the Bacon Dip Mix with the sour cream. Stir until well blended. Cover and refrigerate for at least 1 hour before serving. Serve with chips, crackers or fresh vegetables.

# Onion Cheese Dip Mix

2 T. minced onion
1 tsp. beef bouillon granules
2 T. Parmesan cheese
1/2 tsp. garlic salt

Combine the above ingredients and stir until well blended. Place in a 3" x 4" ziplock bag and seal.

Attach a gift tag with the directions on how to prepare the dip.

# Onion Cheese Dip

**1 pkg. Onion Cheese Dip Mix**
**2 C. sour cream**

Combine the Onion Cheese Dip Mix with the sour cream. Stir until well blended. Cover and refrigerate for at least 1 hour before serving. Serve with chips, crackers or fresh vegetables.

# Garlic Onion Dip Mix

1 T. garlic powder
1 T. onion powder
1 1/2 T. dried parsley
1/2 tsp. salt-free seasoning blend
1/8 tsp. salt

Combine the above ingredients and stir until well blended. Place in a 3" x 4" ziplock bag and seal.

Attach a gift tag with the directions on how to prepare the dip.

# Garlic Onion Dip

1 pkg. Garlic Onion Dip Mix
2 C. sour cream

Combine the Garlic Onion Dip Mix with the sour cream. Stir until well blended. Cover and refrigerate for at least 1 hour before serving. Dip is better if made 8 hours before serving. Serve with chips, crackers or fresh vegetables.

# Creamy Curry Dip Mix

1 T. dried parsley
2 tsp. minced onion
2 tsp. dried chives
1 1/2 tsp. garlic powder
1 tsp. onion powder
1/4 tsp. plus 1/8 tsp. celery salt
1/4 tsp. plus 1/8 tsp. celery seed

1/4 tsp. plus 1/8 tsp. curry
1/8 tsp. turmeric
1/8 tsp. cumin
1/2 tsp. salt

Combine the above ingredients and stir until well blended. Place in a 3" x 4" ziplock bag and seal.

Attach a gift tag with the directions on how to prepare the dip.

# Creamy Curry Dip

1 pkg. Creamy Curry Dip Mix
2 C. sour cream

Combine the Creamy Curry Dip Mix with the sour cream. Stir until well blended. Cover and refrigerate for at least 2 hours before serving. Serve with chips, crackers or fresh vegetables.

# Creamy Curry Dip

1 pkg. Creamy Curry Dip Mix
2 C. sour cream

Combine the Creamy Curry Dip Mix with the sour cream. Stir until well blended. Cover and refrigerate for at least 2 hours before serving. Serve with chips, crackers or fresh vegetables.

To make radish spinner garnishes, trim off the radish's top and bottom. Then cut two 1/8" thick slices. Cut each slice from the center to the outside. Gently push the two slices together where they have been cut at a right angle to form a spinner.

- - - - - - fold - - - - - -

# Creamy Curry Dip

1 pkg. Creamy Curry Dip Mix
2 C. sour cream

Combine the Creamy Curry Dip Mix with the sour cream. Stir until well blended. Cover and refrigerate for at least 2 hours before serving. Serve with chips, crackers or fresh vegetables.

For a fall party, serve dips in small hollowed-out pumpkins. Line the inside with plastic wrap before adding the dip.

- - - - fold - - - - - - - - - - - -

# Chili Cheese & Bacon Dip Mix

1 T. plus 3/4 tsp. minced onion
2 1/2 tsp. bacon bits
1 1/4 tsp. garlic powder
2 1/2 tsp. Cheddar cheese powder
1 1/4 tsp. chili powder
1/2 tsp. cumin
1/4 tsp. cayenne pepper
1/4 tsp. salt

Combine the above ingredients and stir until well blended. Place in a 3" x 4" ziplock bag and seal.

Attach a gift tag with the directions on how to prepare the dip.

# Chili Cheese & Bacon Dip

1 pkg. Chili Cheese & Bacon Dip Mix
2 C. sour cream

Combine the Chili Cheese & Bacon Dip Mix with the sour cream. Stir until well blended. Cover and refrigerate for at least 2 hours before serving. Serve with chips, crackers or fresh vegetables.

# Hot & Spicy Mexican Dip Mix

1 T. minced onion
1 T. chili powder
1 1/2 tsp. garlic powder
1 1/2 tsp. dried cilantro
1 1/2 tsp. dried parsley
1/2 tsp. cayenne pepper
1/2 tsp. cumin
1/4 tsp. pepper
1/4 tsp. salt

Combine the above ingredients and stir until well blended. Place in a 3" x 4" ziplock bag and seal.

Attach a gift tag with the directions on how to prepare the dip.

# Hot & Spicy Mexican Dip

1 pkg. Hot & Spicy Mexican Dip Mix
1 1/2 C. sour cream

Combine the Hot & Spicy Mexican Dip Mix with the sour cream. Stir until well blended. Cover and refrigerate for at least 2 hours before serving. Serve with chips, crackers or fresh vegetables.

# Spicy Cajun Dip Mix

1 T. Hungarian paprika
3/4 tsp. dried thyme
3/4 tsp. dried oregano
3/4 tsp. onion powder
1/2 tsp. cayenne pepper
1/2 tsp. garlic powder
1/4 tsp. pepper
1/4 tsp. sugar

Combine the above ingredients and stir until well blended. Place in a 3" x 4" ziplock bag and seal.

Attach a gift tag with the directions on how to prepare the dip.

# Spicy Cajun Dip

**1 pkg. Spicy Cajun Dip Mix**
**2 C. sour cream**

Combine the Spicy Cajun Dip Mix with the sour cream. Stir until well blended. Cover and refrigerate for at least 8 hours before serving. Serve with chips, crackers or fresh vegetables.

# Veggie Dip Mix

1 T. dried chives
1 tsp. garlic salt
1/2 tsp. dried dill weed
1/2 tsp. paprika

Combine the above ingredients and stir until well blended. Place in a 3" x 4" ziplock bag and seal.

Attach a gift tag with the directions on how to prepare the dip.

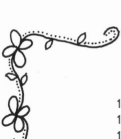

# Veggie Dip

1 pkg. Veggie Dip Mix
1 T. lemon juice
2 C. sour cream

Combine the Veggie Dip Mix with the lemon juice and sour cream. Stir until well blended. Cover and refrigerate for at least 1 hour before serving. Serve with chips, crackers or fresh vegetables.

# Tangy Onion Dip Mix

4 T. minced onion
1 T. sugar
1 T. beef bouillon granules

Combine the above ingredients and stir until well blended. Place in a 3" x 4" ziplock bag and seal.

Attach a gift tag with the directions on how to prepare the dip.

# Tangy Onion Dip

1 pkg. Tangy Onion Dip Mix
1 C. sour cream

Combine the Tangy Onion Dip Mix with the sour cream. Stir until well blended. Cover and refrigerate for at least 2 hours before serving. Serve with chips, crackers or fresh vegetables.

# Savory Herb Cheese Spread Mix

1/4 tsp. minced garlic
4 tsp. dried parsley
4 tsp. dried dill weed
4 tsp. dried basil

Combine the above ingredients and stir until well blended. Place in a 3" x 4" ziplock bag and seal.

Attach a gift tag with the directions on how to prepare the spread.

# Savory Herb Cheese Spread

1 pkg. Savory Herb Cheese Spread Mix
1 (8 oz.) pkg. cream cheese, softened
1/2 tsp. prepared mustard
1/2 tsp. Worcestershire sauce
1/4 C. chopped black olives
1 1/2 T. lemon juice

Combine the Savory Herb Cheese Spread Mix with cream cheese, mustard, Worcestershire sauce, olives and lemon juice. Stir until well blended. Cover and refrigerate for at least 2 hours before serving. Serve with crackers.

# Herb & Garlic Cheese Spread Mix

2 1/4 tsp. dried dill weed
1 1/2 tsp. dried thyme
3/4 tsp. dried oregano
3/4 tsp. garlic powder
3/4 tsp. pepper
3/4 tsp. seasoned salt

Combine the above ingredients and stir until well blended. Place in a 3" x 4" ziplock bag and seal.

Attach a gift tag with the directions on how to prepare the spread.

# Herb & Garlic Cheese Spread

1 pkg. Herb & Garlic Cheese Spread Mix
3 (8 oz.) pkgs. cream cheese, softened
1 1/2 C. butter, softened

Combine the Herb & Garlic Cheese Spread Mix with cream cheese and butter. Stir until well blended. Cover and refrigerate for at least 2 hours before serving. Serve with crackers.